My Farm

My Chickens

By Heather Miller

Welcome
Books

Children's Press
A Division of Grolier Publishing
New York / London / Hong Kong / Sydney
Danbury, Connecticut

Photo Credits: Cover and pp. 5, 7, 9, 11, 13, 15, 21 by Thaddeus Harden; p. 17 © Julie Habel/Corbis; p. 19 © James Marshall/Corbis

Contributing Editor: Jennifer Ceaser
Book Design: MaryJane Wojciechowski

Visit Children's Press on the Internet at:
http://publishing.grolier.com

Library of Congress Cataloging-in-Publication Data

Miller, Heather.
  My chickens / by Heather Miller.
    p. cm. — (My farm)
  Includes bibliographical references and index.
  Summary: A young girl describes how she cares for the chickens living on her farm.
  ISBN 0-516-23105-7 (lib. bdg.) — ISBN 0-516-23030-1 (pbk.)
  1. Chickens—Juvenile literature. [1. Chickens.] I. Title.

SF487.5.M53 2000
636.5—dc21
                                                          00-024385

Contents

1 "COCK-A-DOODLE-DOO!" 4

2 Feeding My Chickens 10

3 Gathering Eggs 12

4 A Special Kind of Egg 16

5 New Words 22

6 To Find Out More 23

7 Index 24

8 About the Author 24

"COCK-A-DOODLE-DOO!"

"COCK-A-DOODLE-DOO!"

What is making that loud sound so early in the morning?

4

5

It is my **rooster** making that loud sound!

My rooster is **crowing**.

My rooster always crows early in the morning.

7

It is time to feed my chickens.

I go to the chicken **coop**.

A coop is where chickens live.

I feed my chickens every morning.

I feed my chickens **grain**.

I **pour** the grain on the ground.

My **hens** lay eggs every day.

Only hens can lay eggs.

I gather the eggs in a basket.

13

I bring the eggs to the kitchen.

My dad cooks them for breakfast.

14

One of my hens lays a special kind of egg.

These eggs are left in her nest.

Soon the eggs **hatch**.

Out comes a **chick**!

A chick is a baby chicken.

Chickens spend the day outside.

They go back in the coop at the end of the day.

Goodnight, my chickens!

21

New Words

chick (**chik**) a baby chicken

coop (**koop**) a place where chickens live

crowing (**kroh**-ing) the sound that a rooster makes

grain (**grayn**) a kind of food chickens eat

hatch (**hatch**) when an egg opens up and a chick comes out

hens (**henz**) female chickens

pour (**por**) to make something flow

22 **rooster** (**ru**-ster) a male chicken

To Find Out More

Books

Chickens
by Peter Brady
Capstone Press

From Egg to Chicken (Lifecycles)
by Gerard Legg and Carolyn Scrace
Franklin Watts

Too Many Chickens
by Paulette Bourgeois
Kids Can Press

Web Site
Kids Farm
http://www.kidsfarm.com
Learn all about different kinds of farm animals,
including chickens.

Index

chick, 18

coop, 8

crowing, 6

hatch, 18

hens, 12, 16

rooster, 6

grain, 10

pour, 10

About the Author

Heather Miller lives in Cambridge, Massachusetts, with her son, Jasper. She is a graduate student at Harvard University.

Reading Consultants

Kris Flynn, Coordinator, Small School District Literacy, The San Diego County Office of Education

Shelly Forys, Certified Reading Recovery Specialist, W.J. Zahnow Elementary School, Waterloo, IL

Peggy McNamara, Professor, Bank Street College of Education, Reading and Literacy Program